W9-AEK-867

TECHNOLOGY

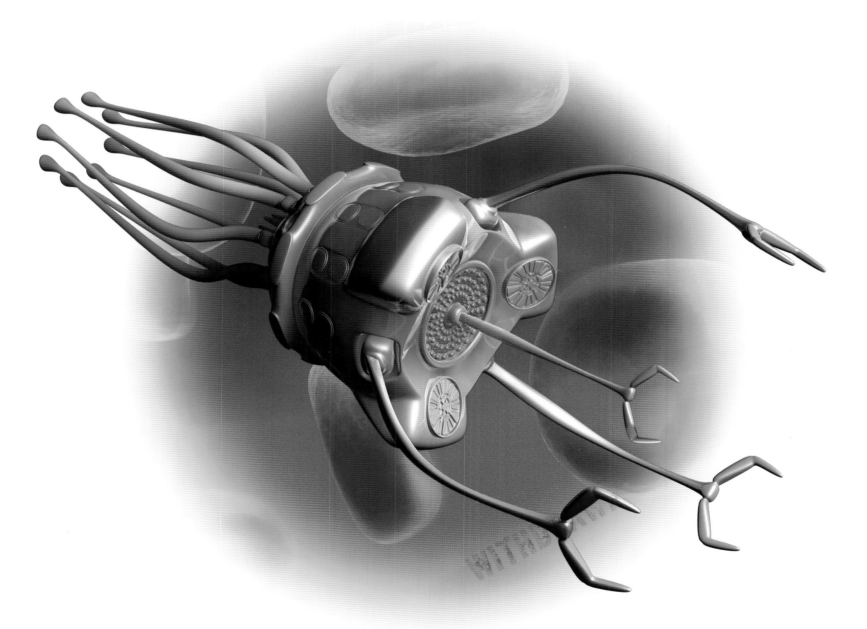

Peter Kent

KINGFISHER
NEW YORK

Jefferson Madison
Regional Library
Charlottesville, Virginia

30476 2493
A

KINGFISHER
LONDON & NEW YORK

Copyright © 2009 by Kingfisher
Published in the United States by Kingfisher,
175 Fifth Ave., New York, NY 10010
Kingfisher is an imprint of Macmillan Children's Books, London.
All rights reserved.

Illustrations by McKoen Productions and Sebastian Quigley

Distributed in the U.S. by Macmillan, 175 Fifth Ave., New York, NY 10010
Distributed in Canada by H.B. Fenn and Company Ltd., 34 Nixon Road, Bolton, Ontario L7E 1W2

Library of Congress Cataloging-in-Publication data has been applied for.

ISBN: 978-0-7534-6307-9

Kingfisher books are available for special promotions and premiums. For details contact: Special Markets
Department, Macmillan, 175 Fifth Avenue, New York, NY 10010.

For more information, please visit www.kingfisherpublications.com

Printed in Taiwan
1 3 5 7 9 8 6 4 2
1TR/0509/SHENS/SC/126.6MA/C

Note to readers: The website addresses listed in this book are correct at the time of publishing.
However, due to the ever-changing nature of the Internet, website addresses and content can change.
Websites can contain links that are unsuitable for children. The publisher cannot be held responsible for
changes in website addresses or content or for information obtained through third-party websites.
We strongly advise that Internet searches are supervised by an adult.

The Publisher would like to thank the following for permission to reproduce their images (t = top, b = bottom, c = centre, r = right, l = left):

Front cover Shutterstock/DarkGeometryStudios; back cover Shutterstock/Stefan Glebowski; page 1 Sebastian Quigley; 2–3 Rob McKoen;
4–5 Sebastian Quigley; 4br Corbis/Geoff Renner/Robert Harding Picture Library; 5cr Science Photo Library (SPL)/Pasieka; 6–7 Rob McKoen;
8–9 Sebastian Quigley; 9t Getty/AFP; 9b Sebastian Quigley; 10–11 Rob McKoen; 11c Reuters; 11r Reuters; 12–13 Rob McKoen; 13b Sebastian
Quigley; 14–15 Reproduced with the very kind permission of Virgin Galactic; 16–17 Sebastian Quigley; 16c SPL/OME; 18–19 Rob McKoen with
the very kind permission of Pelamis Wave Power Ltd.; 19br PA/AP/Finavera; 20–21 Rob McKoen; 21br Shutterstock/Tatonka; 22–23 Rob McKoen;
23b Sebastian Quigley; 24tl Reproduced with the very kind permission of Stirling Energy Systems Inc.; 24br Sebastian Quigley; 25 PA/AP; 26–27
Sebastian Quigley; 27 NASA Dryden Flight Research Center; 28–29 Sebastian Quigley; 28cl Corbis/George Steinmetz; 28c Shutterstock/Elmantas
Buzas; 29cl Shutterstock/Stephen Van Horn; 30–31 Rob McKoen; 30b Sebastian Quigley; 32–33 Shutterstock/photobank.klev.ua; 32cl SPL/Andrew
Syed; 32c Shutterstock/Cathleen Clapper; 32bl Shutterstock/STILLFX; 33t Shutterstock/Sune Falk; 33cr Shutterstock/Arvind Balaraman;
33bl Shutterstock/PopArt; 33bc Shutterstock/Jostein Hauge; 33br Shutterstock/Andrea Leone; 34–35 Sebastian Quigley; 35 Reproduced
with the very kind permission of Vecna Technologies Inc.; 35c Reuters; 36–37 Shutterstock/Sebastian Kaulitzki; 36–37 Sebastian Quigley;
36bl SPL/David McCarthy; 36br Reproduced with the very kind permission of Lizardfire Studios; 38–39 Kobal; 38all Kobal; 39tc Sebastian
Quigley; 39bl & br Ronald Grant Archive; 40l Mike Davis; 40–41 Rob McKoen; 41b Getty/Juan Ocampo; 42–43 Photolibrary/Chad Ehlers;
43b Corbis/Noah K. Murray; 48tr Getty/AFP; 48cl Corbis/Rune Hellestad; 48cr PA/Katsumi Kashara; 48bl PA/Salvatore di Nolfi

CONTENTS

4 WORLD MACHINE

6 MEGATUNNEL

8 SUPERBRIDGE

10 ENGINE ROOM

12 ROCKET SCIENCE

14 SPACE TOURS

16 SPACE ELEVATOR

18 WAVE FARMING

20 PARTICLE POWER

22 NUCLEAR POWERED

24 SOLAR FARMING

26 SOLAR SAILING

28 GPS

30 ECOHOME

32 DIGIWORLD

34 ROBOT RESCUE

36 NANOBOTS

38 SFX

40 GRAPHIC GAMES

42 FUN MACHINE

44 GLOSSARY

46 INDEX

48 INVESTIGATE

FOSSIL FUEL—a fuel, such as coal or natural gas, that is obtained from fossilized remains in the earth

WORLD MACHINE

Earth is not a dead rock. It is like a complicated, gigantic machine. Every machine needs power to work, and Earth gets all it needs from the Sun. The Sun drives the planet's climate, winds, and waves, and beneath Earth's surface is a molten core—another source of heat and power. Much of today's technology is in some way linked to these basic resources.

Offshore turbines convert wind energy into electrical power.

Rigs out at sea are used to extract oil and gas fuel from beneath the ocean.

Water technology

The ocean covers about one-third of the planet, so making use of its potential is vital. Water and waves can be used to drive generators as a way of producing electrical power without polluting the atmosphere.

wave farm off the coast of Portugal (*see page 18*)

Water drives electricity generators at hydroelectric power plants.

Geothermal power

Heat stored under the ground can be tapped for power. In some places there are natural springs of hot water, but usually a hole is drilled down to hot rock. Water is pumped down the hole. This water turns to steam, which shoots up to power a turbine and a generator. Geothermal power plants do not need any fuel, nor do they produce any harmful gases.

geothermal power plant in New Zealand

"The world, like any other machine, doesn't need a spanner in the works."

Fred Hoyle (1915–2001)
British astronomer

www.brainpop.com/technology

geothermal power plant

GPS (Global Positioning System) satellites circle Earth (see page 28).

Engineering technology

Amazing bridges, tunnels, and vehicles enable people to travel from place to place more quickly than ever, while satellites in space help us find our way around the planet.

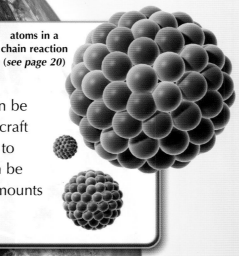

atoms in a chain reaction (*see page 20*)

Particle technology

The tiniest particles can be used to propel a spacecraft through space, or split to release energy that can be converted into huge amounts of electrical power.

⊝ NEW MATERIALS

In the 21st century, scientists are creating materials that do not occur in nature. These are composites (mixtures) made of different elements, designed to be very strong and light. Carbon nanotubes are the strongest materials yet known. Lighter than hair, they are tougher than a diamond.

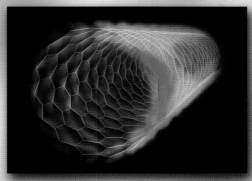

computer-generated artwork of a carbon nanotube (*see pages 16 and 36*)

Solar farms capture the power of the Sun (see page 24).

a solar sail (*see page 26*)

Solar technology

The Sun's energy can be harnessed to power cars, planes, spacecraft, and other vehicles. To help reduce our use of fossil fuels, which will one day run out, it is also used to heat homes and provide electricity.

a game character, created and animated by computer software (*see page 40*)

Digital technology

Technology can also be fun. Advances in digital gaming and the Internet mean that we can now play games with people living on the other side of the planet.

Conveyor belts

The small chips of rock are carried away on a conveyor belt powered by electric motors. If the belt is not close enough to the tunnel entrance, it transfers the debris to railroad trucks, which haul it away.

Tunnel segments

The tunnels are lined to prevent pieces of rock from breaking off or, in softer ground, to stop the tunnel from collapsing. The lining is made of concrete segments, which fit together to form a ring. The segments are pushed into place with pneumatic rams.

There are usually five to eight segments in each ring, plus a smaller "key" piece.

MEGA -TUNNEL

Tunnels are very expensive to build, but they speed up journeys by reducing the distance a vehicle has to travel from place to place. There are thousands of miles of tunnels in the world, through mountains, under rivers, and even beneath the sea. These days most are created by huge tunnel-boring machines (TBMs). TBMs make tunneling faster and safer than in the days when miners had only shovels, drills, and explosives.

Pneumatic jacks

Powerful pneumatic jacks, or rams, press against the side walls to change the direction of tunneling. Other jacks push against the last ring of segments to propel the TBM forward.

> The Rock of Gibraltar is like a honeycomb—37 mi. (60km) of tunnels have been dug there.

A mechanical worm

In nature, a shipworm bores through wood, which then passes through its body. A TBM is a mechanical version of this sea creature. It is a metal tube full of machinery, weighing thousands of tons. At the front, a rotating disk cuts into the rock, which is passed through the disk and then back through the machine on a conveyor belt. The tube reinforces the tunnel roof while a strong lining is fitted. Powerful pneumatic jacks push the machine forward.

operators in the control cabin

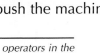

Alpine tunnel

The new Gotthard railroad tunnel in Switzerland (shown in yellow) is much straighter and deeper than the older, more winding route it is replacing (shown in red). It will make the journey between Italy and Switzerland, through the Alps, much shorter and quicker.

When it is finished, in 2015, the 35-mi. (57-km)-long Gotthard Base Tunnel will be the longest in the world.

Switzerland

Italy

www.oobject.com/20-interesting-boring-machines

Cutting disk

The cutter head acts like an enormous cheese grater, scraping off the rock by using rows of cutting disks made from very tough steel. The disks wear down quickly and have to be changed. In very hard rock this might be as often as once every 1,640 ft. (500m).

Direction and speed

An operator drives and steers the TBM. Laser beams make sure it is always heading on the correct path. The average speed of a TBM, depending on the type of rock, is about 28 in. (70cm) per hour—about 50 times slower

HYDRAULIC—operated by the pressurized movement of water, or other fluid, carried through pipes

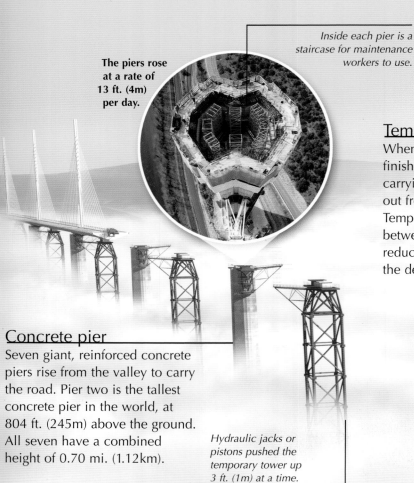

The piers rose at a rate of 13 ft. (4m) per day.

Inside each pier is a staircase for maintenance workers to use.

Temporary pier

When the concrete piers were finished, the steel decks for carrying the road were pushed out from either side of the valley. Temporary steel piers were built between the concrete ones to reduce the distance over which the deck had to be supported.

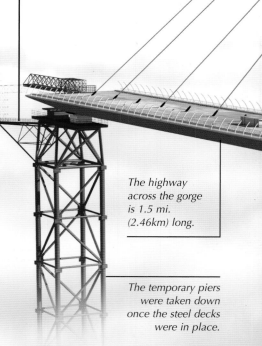

Concrete pier

Seven giant, reinforced concrete piers rise from the valley to carry the road. Pier two is the tallest concrete pier in the world, at 804 ft. (245m) above the ground. All seven have a combined height of 0.70 mi. (1.12km).

Hydraulic jacks or pistons pushed the temporary tower up 3 ft. (1m) at a time.

The highway across the gorge is 1.5 mi. (2.46km) long.

The temporary piers were taken down once the steel decks were in place.

SUPERBRIDGE

Up until 200 years ago, bridges were made only of stone, brick, and wood, which limited their size. The use of iron and steel, from the 1800s onward, made bigger bridges possible. Today, lightweight steel and other extra-strong materials allow engineers to build enormous bridges, capable of spanning seas as well as rivers and valleys. The Millau Viaduct in France (above) is an impressive example. There are even plans to bridge the Strait of Gibraltar so that people can drive directly from Europe to Africa.

The Millau Viaduct

This awe-inspiring structure spans the deep, wide gorge of the Tarn River in southern France, allowing a highway to reach the Mediterranean Sea. It is the tallest bridge ever built. It took ten years to plan and just over three to construct. The bridge was opened in December 2004. It cost 300 million euros (about $390 million) and, thankfully, not a single human life.

> The tallest mast top along the Millau Viaduct is 1,125 ft. (343m) above the river—higher than the top of the Eiffel Tower in Paris.

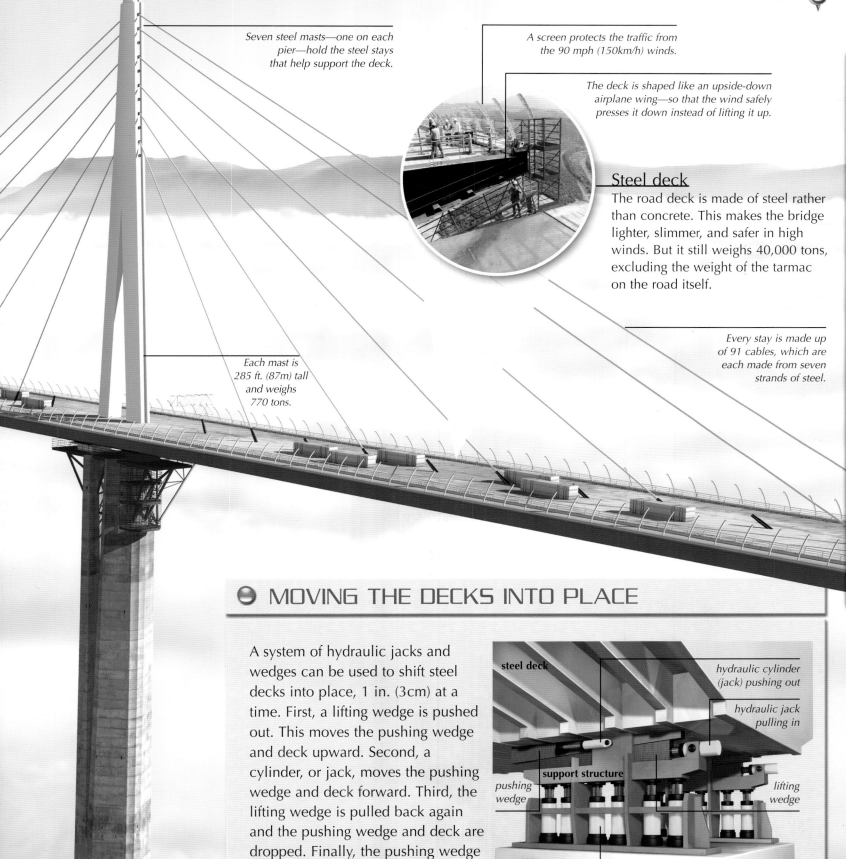

Seven steel masts—one on each pier—hold the steel stays that help support the deck.

A screen protects the traffic from the 90 mph (150km/h) winds.

The deck is shaped like an upside-down airplane wing—so that the wind safely presses it down instead of lifting it up.

Steel deck

The road deck is made of steel rather than concrete. This makes the bridge lighter, slimmer, and safer in high winds. But it still weighs 40,000 tons, excluding the weight of the tarmac on the road itself.

Each mast is 285 ft. (87m) tall and weighs 770 tons.

Every stay is made up of 91 cables, which are each made from seven strands of steel.

⊖ MOVING THE DECKS INTO PLACE

A system of hydraulic jacks and wedges can be used to shift steel decks into place, 1 in. (3cm) at a time. First, a lifting wedge is pushed out. This moves the pushing wedge and deck upward. Second, a cylinder, or jack, moves the pushing wedge and deck forward. Third, the lifting wedge is pulled back again and the pushing wedge and deck are dropped. Finally, the pushing wedge is moved back to its original position to repeat the first pushing action.

steel deck

hydraulic cylinder (jack) pushing out

hydraulic jack pulling in

support structure

pushing wedge

lifting wedge

concrete pier

balancing cylinder

ENGINE ROOM

WHEEL TRUCK—the swivelling undercarriage of a locomotive or carriage, with two or more pairs of wheels

For a trip of less than 300 mi. (500km), the electric train is quicker than an airplane or a car and also produces fewer greenhouse gases. It is quieter than a plane, and the track takes up less room than an airport or expressway. In 1960, Japan stunned the world by building a new line between Osaka and Tokyo, with electric trains speeding at an amazing 137 mph (220km/h). The French went one better in the 1980s— their high-speed TGV trains can travel in excess of 186 mph (300km/h).

The wheel truck

Six wheel trucks power a TGV train: three at each end. Each has two 1,000-horsepower electric motors connected to the axle through gears. Each truck is as powerful as a steam express engine but weighs only as much as a small car.

"It's a pretty toy, but I don't see any use for it."

Michael Faraday (1791–1867)
British scientist, commenting on the world's first electric motor

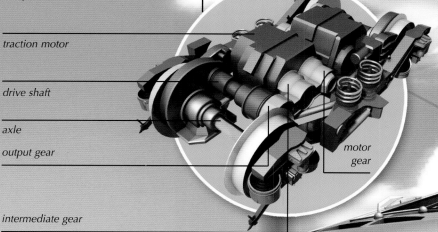

traction motor

drive shaft

axle

output gear

motor gear

intermediate gear

crash-proof driver's cab, with strong anticollision bulkhead

headlights and warning lights

front power car of a high-speed TGV (*train à grande vitesse*)

automatic couplers for joining two TGVs together to run as one

03

TGV power

TGV trains do not need to carry fuel or large engines. Each one has 12 motors, providing a grand total of 12,000 horsepower. That gives very high speed and also fantastic acceleration. In 2007, a TGV set a new world rail speed record of 357 mph (575km/h).

⊖ IN DEVELOPMENT: THE AGV (AUTOMOTRICE À GRANDE VITESSE)

Technicians are developing a new version of the TGV, without the power cars at each end. In an AGV, all the electrical equipment is located under the floor, and the motors are spread out along the train, in wheel trucks between carriages. With no power cars, it is 30 percent lighter than the TGV and has more room for passengers. More power is transmitted directly to the wheels, so the AGV runs even faster while using less energy.

AGV front carriage under construction (left) and its sleek and comfortable driver's cab (above)

www.mos.org/sln/Leonardo/InventorsToolbox.html

All railroad signals are shown on a display inside the cab.

Ventilating grilles prevent the power car from overheating.

circuit breakers and control equipment

The power car
The front carriage has equipment to convert and control energy from the overhead power line. The transformer receives 25,000 volts of electricity and reduces it to 1,500 volts for the motors. A computer makes sure the wheels turn at the right speed, so no power is wasted.

Copper power lines transmit the electric current.

The pantograph is a frame that collects the electric current.

main transformer

railroad tie

The track curves are very gentle, with ballast gravel under the ties, giving a smooth, safe, and speedy ride.

ROCKET SCIENCE

"We'll never be a great civilization as long as rain showers can delay the launch of a space rocket."

George Carlin (1937–2008)
American actor, author, and standup comedian

To get a spacecraft into space, you need powerful rocket engines that can propel it upward at 25,000 mph (40,000km/h), the speed required to blast free of Earth's gravitational pull. But once the craft is in space, there is virtually no gravity and none of the friction forces created by moving through Earth's atmosphere, so very little power is needed to accelerate or change direction. This means a different type of engine can operate in space, using a lighter, more economical fuel.

The fairing, or nose cone, protects the cargo as Soyuz climbs through the atmosphere.

Fregat's engine fires to steer the spacecraft into its final position.

Rocket stage separation
The rocket is built in "stages." Each stage fires its engines until its fuel is all burned up. Then the next stage takes over. The four booster rockets provide most of the power at liftoff. They burn for about two minutes and then break away.

Fregat is a controllable craft used to push the payload (cargo) into its correct orbit.

Stage 3 is 22 ft. (6.7m) long and weighs 25 tons.

Stage 2 is 92 ft. (28m) long and weighs 112 tons.

First stage separation: the four boosters peel off and fall back to Earth

Second stage separation: the central core drops away and burns up as it hits the atmosphere

Soyuz-Fregat

This type of rocket (left) is used to launch satellites and spacecraft into orbit from its launch site in Russia. It stands 139 ft. (42.5m) tall and weighs 330 tons—all except 29 tons of that huge mass is made up of its liquid oxygen and kerosene fuel. More than 1,735 *Soyuz* rockets have been launched since 1966.

Four booster rockets make up Stage 1. Each is 65 ft. (19.8m) long and weighs 46 tons.

> Of all the 300-plus tons that blast into space as part of a *Soyuz* launch, only the 5-ton payload remains there.

The *BepiColombo* spacecraft will be launched in 2013 and is scheduled to reach Mercury in 2019.

Communication dish to receive commands and send back information.

Soyuz can carry a payload of 5.8 tons into space.

http://solarsystem.nasa.gov/kids/ionengines.cfm

The rocket payload

The nose cone of *Soyuz* opens up and is discarded before the engine on the *Fregat* craft fires up. *Fregat*'s engine can be turned on and off to maneuver the payload into its final position. Then the payload separates.

The ion engine's gas fuel is very light, so a large supply of it can be carried onboard—enough for missions lasting years.

Solar panels, once unfolded, will provide the electricity to charge the xenon gas and make the ion engine work.

Ion thrusters

A long-distance spacecraft needs an engine that uses very little and very light fuel—otherwise it would be too heavy for a rocket to carry into orbit. So some spacecraft have an ion engine, which is fueled by particles of xenon gas.

⊖ THE ION ENGINE

An ion engine emits a high-speed stream of xenon gas particles from a nozzle. These particles push the spacecraft forward. The thrust is very gentle—about the same as a piece of paper pressing on your hand. But because there is no resistance in space, this is enough—over time—to propel the craft to speeds of more than 9,900 mph (16,000km/h).

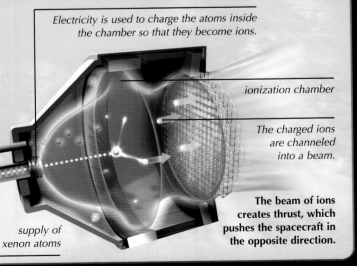

Electricity is used to charge the atoms inside the chamber so that they become ions.

ionization chamber

The charged ions are channeled into a beam.

The beam of ions creates thrust, which pushes the spacecraft in the opposite direction.

supply of xenon atoms

GLIDING—flying without any power for an airplane, the forward motion keeps air flowing over the wings to keep it in the air

Left WK2 cabin is used to view SS2 launch; the one on right is for SS2 training.

SpaceShipTwo (SS2) passenger spacecraft

wingspan of 141 ft. (43m)

The mother ship is called WhiteKnightTwo (WK2).

PW 308A jet engine

Zero-G experience

When there is no gravity, there is no up or down, so the cabin has viewing windows on its roof, sides, and floor. Handhol on the sides of the cabin allow the passengers to move arounc

emergency exit hatch

pilots' cabin

The passenger craft is known as *SpaceShipTwo (SS2).*

SPACE TOURS

A spacecraft has been designed to reach the edge of space, about 60 mi. (100km) above Earth. It will not orbit (circle) the planet like a space station or satellite— but the crew and passengers will actually enter space for a few minutes, and experience weightlessness, before the craft returns to the ground. The two-and-a-half hour voyage will cost passengers about $200,000 for five precious minutes of zero-gravity floating time.

Into orbit

The spaceship is carried up to a height of about 9 mi. (15km) beneath the wings of a mother ship. It flies using four ordinary jet engines. When the passenger spacecraft is released, its rocket engine fires and blasts it up to an amazing 68 mi. (110km), at 1,550 mph (2,500km/h)—about the speed of the fastest jet fighters. The engine cuts out so that the craft coasts for the last few thousand yards, hanging in space for a few minutes.

 > These vehicles (above) are based on the spacecraft designs that won a competition known as the X Prize in 2004.

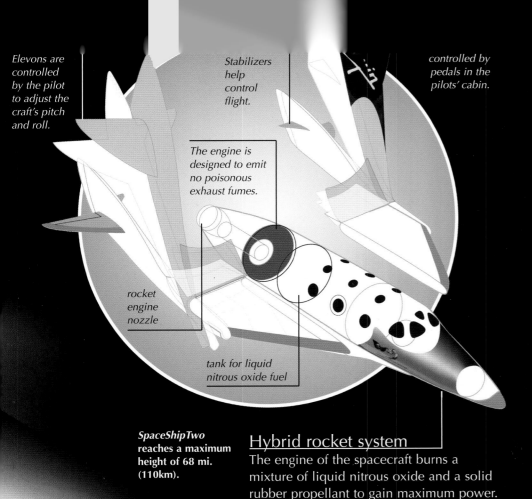

Elevons are controlled by the pilot to adjust the craft's pitch and roll.

Stabilizers help control flight.

controlled by pedals in the pilots' cabin.

The engine is designed to emit no poisonous exhaust fumes.

rocket engine nozzle

tank for liquid nitrous oxide fuel

SpaceShipTwo reaches a maximum height of 68 mi. (110km).

Hybrid rocket system

The engine of the spacecraft burns a mixture of liquid nitrous oxide and a solid rubber propellant to gain maximum power. It burns for only 90 seconds. Other than turning the engine on and off, the pilot has no control over it.

◉ THE SPACEPORT

The flights will take off from Spaceport America in Upham, New Mexico. The new terminal looks a little like a spacecraft itself—designed by Norman Foster, who also worked on the Millau Viaduct (*see pages 8–9*). To make it as ecologically friendly as possible, the spaceport is partially buried under the ground to keep it cool by day and warm at night.

For now, only one space flight from the port will be scheduled per day.

www.spaceadventures.com

Return trip

When the rocket engine runs out of fuel, the rear wings lift up. This slows the spacecraft to 186 mph (300km/h) as it glides back to Earth. It reenters the atmosphere at a much slower speed than other spacecraft, building up less friction, so it does not risk burning up during reentry.

The spacecraft drops down to 14 mi. (23km)—then the wings extend and it begins to glide.

Passenger spacecraft

The spacecraft is as big as a medium-sized executive jet or a small bus. It has seats for two pilots and six passengers. The cabin was designed to allow the passengers to float around freely during their five minutes of weightlessness.

The spacecraft slowly glides down to land at the spaceport.

Elevator car

Passengers and cargo will be carried inside an elevator car that will climb up the ribbon to a space station orbiting the planet. Unlike an ordinary elevator, which is pulled up by cables, the space elevator will climb the ribbon with grips or rollers, a lot like a koala using its claws to climb up a tree. Photoelectric cells on the outside will convert a laser beam, transmitted from below, into electrical power for the elevator car.

The passenger car will have to be pressurized, like the cabin of a spacecraft, so that those onboard can breathe.

Carbon-based material is 20 times lighter than steel and 180 times as strong.

Carbon nanotubes

An extremely strong and light material will be needed to create a wire capable of supporting the space elevator. Carbon nanotubes could be the solution. Carbon is a very strong element and can be arranged to form tiny threads that are only one nanometer thick.

> NANOMETER (NM)—*1nm is equal to one billionth of a meter*

SPACE ELEVATOR

Rockets are a very expensive—and dangerous—way of carrying things into space. The journey would be much simpler if there were a tower or elevator that people could use to climb into orbit. A tower built of ordinary materials would be too heavy to stand upright. But scientists and engineers are working on a way to attach a wire to a satellite, orbiting Earth, so that an elevator can travel up it. To achieve this, the wire, or ribbon, would need to be attached to a counterweight (see diagram, below).

"The space elevator will be built about 50 years after everyone stops laughing."

Arthur C. Clarke (1917–2008)
British science-fiction author and inventor

A DIRECT ROUTE INTO SPACE

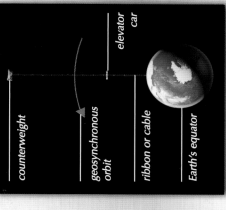

counterweight

elevator car

geosynchronous orbit

ribbon or cable

Earth's equator

The ribbon would extend from Earth 22 mi. (35.6km) up to a station or satellite traveling on a "geosynchronous" orbit. This means the station remains above the same spot as it goes around Earth. Beyond the station, the ribbon would run out into space for almost 62,000 mi. (100,000km) with its end attached to a large weight—possibly a small captured asteroid. As the counterweight goes around Earth, it would pull the ribbon to keep it tightly stretched out.

A laser beam, focused by mirrors, provides electrical power for the elevator car as it travels into space.

Base station

The ribbon will be anchored on Earth at a base station. Here, a power station will focus a laser beam up to the elevator as a source of electrical power. The base station will have to be on or very close to the equator, where Earth moves the fastest. This will help keep the ribbon pulled tight.

> For return trips, the elevator car could be detached from the ribbon to fly down through Earth's atmosphere like a space shuttle does.

The first-ever working wave farm, shown here, was moored off the coast of Portugal in 2006.

PISTON—a tube-shaped device that moves up and down to pump fluid around inside a machine or engine

"Sea snake" generators

Sausage-shaped trains of steel cylinders are anchored to the ocean floor, facing the direction of the waves as they roll into shore. Each one is 460 ft. (140m) long and divided into three sections. As the waves move up and down, the sections bend at their hinged joints. The moving joints drive hydraulic motors inside, and this powers generators that make electricity.

Joints and hinges

The joints of the units are the most important parts. The cylinders in between are simply hollow tubes to keep the whole system afloat. Each joint has a hinge connecting it to a smaller cylinder that contains the power-generating equipment.

buoyancy cylinder

There are three generating units in each train of cylinders.

WAVE FARMING

The ocean has the greatest potential supply of renewable energy in the world—and in recent years, scientists and engineers have developed new ways of harvesting the power of waves. Water is 1,000 times more dense than air, so its potential energy is very much greater than that of wind. Power generated from waves will never run out and does not send any greenhouse gases into the atmosphere. It is the ultimate green—or "blue"—fuel.

Junction boxes

The electric current produced by each unit is carried down cables to a junction box on the seabed. This connects the lines from all three generators to the main power cable that carries the electricity from the wave farm to the shore.

> Depending on how rough the ocean is, each generator can provide electrical power for up to 500 homes.

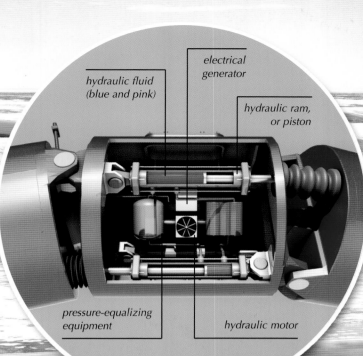

hydraulic fluid
(blue and pink)

electrical
generator

hydraulic ram,
or piston

pressure-equalizing
equipment

hydraulic motor

Hydraulic pump and motor

This unit converts the wave motion into electricity. As the sections on either side move up and down on the waves, they push hydraulic rams backward and forward. The two rams always work in opposite directions, pumping fluid through a small hydraulic motor to turn an electrical generator.

www.pelamiswave.com

"When I see a mighty wave beating the shore, I think of a great horse idly pawing the grass and long to set it in harness."

Sir George Sydenham Clarke (1848–1933)
British military engineer

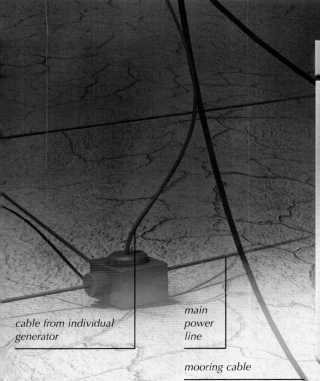

cable from individual
generator

main
power
line

mooring cable

⊖ HOW AN AQUABUOY WORKS

An "aquabuoy" can also generate power from the waves. A long, open-ended steel tube hangs down from a floating buoy. As the waves move, the water pushes a piston up and down inside the tube. This forces water through a high-pressure pump to drive a turbine, which then turns a generator to make electricity.

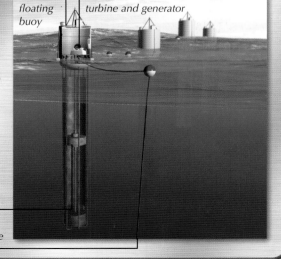

floating
buoy

turbine and generator

piston

power line to shore

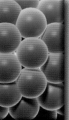

PARTICLE POWER

Nuclear power is one way of creating a lot of energy without releasing harmful greenhouse gases into the atmosphere. Sadly, the process is expensive and potentially hazardous—the safety costs are high, and the dangerous waste products must be stored safely for many years while their radioactivity dies away. But for many people, the power contained inside tiny atoms is the answer to our future energy needs.

NEUTRON—a particle with no electrical charge which makes up an atom along with protons and electrons

A nuclear plant

A nuclear power plant consists of three basic units: the reactor that creates heat and steam, a turbine driven by the steam, and a generator, powered by the turbine, that makes electricity. To make the process as safe as possible, all the machinery must be built to the highest standards. The risk of anything failing, exploding, or leaking is kept as small as possible.

SPLITTING AN ATOM

1. A single neutron is fired into the unstable nucleus of an atom.

3. The new neutrons shoot off to split more nuclei and release more energy and neutrons. This is a chain reaction.

2. The nucleus splits in two. As it does so, it releases energy and additional neutrons.

The splitting process (above) is known as nuclear fission.

All things are made up of tiny particles called atoms, and in the center of every atom is a nucleus. When a nucleus is split, a tiny amount of the energy that holds the atom together is released. When billions of atoms are split, the energy created is enormous. This can be released as a controlled and constant supply of useful energy known as a chain reaction.

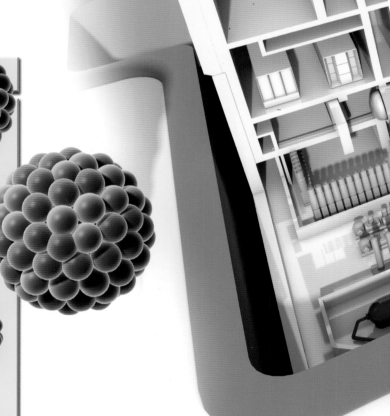

"Whoever talks about getting power on an industrial scale from splitting the atom is talking moonshine."

Ernest Rutherford (1871–1937)
scientist from New Zealand

 > The energy in a lump of uranium the size of a sugar cube is enough to power a submarine across the Atlantic Ocean.

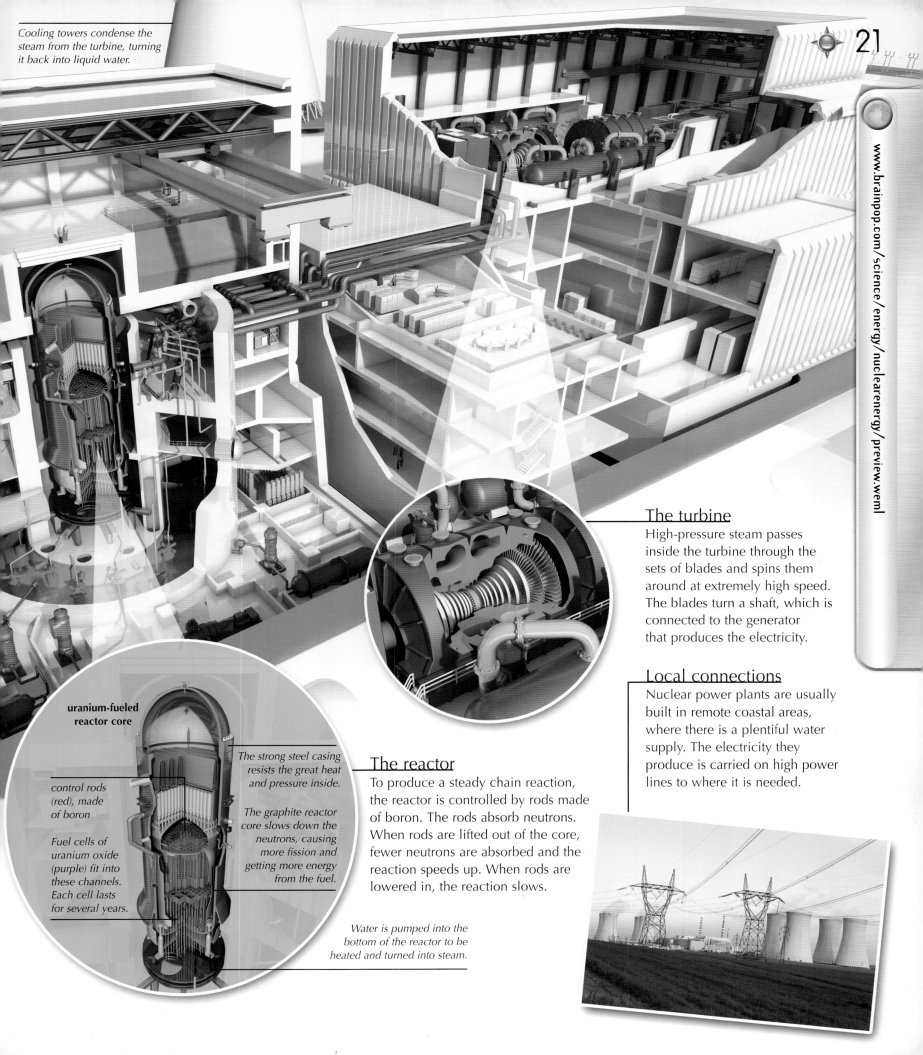

Cooling towers condense the steam from the turbine, turning it back into liquid water.

www.brainpop.com/science/energy/nuclearenergy/preview.weml

The turbine

High-pressure steam passes inside the turbine through the sets of blades and spins them around at extremely high speed. The blades turn a shaft, which is connected to the generator that produces the electricity.

Local connections

Nuclear power plants are usually built in remote coastal areas, where there is a plentiful water supply. The electricity they produce is carried on high power lines to where it is needed.

uranium-fueled reactor core

The strong steel casing resists the great heat and pressure inside.

control rods (red), made of boron

The graphite reactor core slows down the neutrons, causing more fission and getting more energy from the fuel.

Fuel cells of uranium oxide (purple) fit into these channels. Each cell lasts for several years.

The reactor

To produce a steady chain reaction, the reactor is controlled by rods made of boron. The rods absorb neutrons. When rods are lifted out of the core, fewer neutrons are absorbed and the reaction speeds up. When rods are lowered in, the reaction slows.

Water is pumped into the bottom of the reactor to be heated and turned into steam.

NUCLEAR POWERED

A nuclear-powered submarine can stay deep and hidden underwater for as long as it needs to—without having to surface to recharge. It could stay submerged for years before the reactor needed to be refueled, but that might damage the health of the crew onboard. As long as the sailors remain physically and mentally fit and have adequate supplies, there are few reasons to visit the surface.

BALLAST—a heavy material put aboard a ship to make it stable in the water, or in a submarine to make it submerge (sink)

The periscope, radio, radar, and direction-finding antennae are painted with irregular patterns to make them difficult to see.

Ohio-class submarine

Each carrying 24 Trident nuclear missiles, the 18 submarines of the "Ohio class" are the biggest in the mighty U.S. Navy. Their nuclear-powered engines allow them to lie hidden in the ocean for months at a time, always armed and ready to strike.

The fin, or sail, serves as a mount for the periscopes and antennae and as an observation platform when the submarine surfaces.

Diving planes tilt up and down to increase the speed of diving and to control depth when underwater.

The very strong inner pressure hull, 3 in. (75mm) thick, contains all the living quarters and machinery spaces.

Crew quarters

Each underwater mission lasts for about three months, so the 155 crew members are given very comfortable quarters, with good food and entertainment.

Sonar

A submarine "sees" through its sonar (*s*ound *n*avigation *a*nd *r*anging) equipment. This equipment sends out a noise that bounces back if it hits an object. Computers then figure out the size, distance, and direction of the object.

The sonar dome, or boom, which emits pulses of sound, is located in the bow (front end) of the submarine.

 ⟩ The first submarine to be powered by a nuclear reactor was the USS *Nautilus*, launched in 1955.

Inside the reactor chamber

A small but very powerful nuclear reactor generates a lot of heat. A circuit of water under high pressure passes through the reactor and is turned into steam. The steam drives a turbine, which powers the propeller and a generator that makes electricity for the systems onboard.

sealed reactor chamber

The rudder steers the submarine from side to side.

http://americanhistory.si.edu/subs/index.html

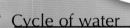

The propeller has seven blades, specially designed to make as little noise as possible.

Cycle of water

The steam is condensed—cooled and changed back into liquid water—and returned to the reactor vessel, where it is reheated. This process can go on for as long as the reactor remains active and the machinery does not wear out.

The drive shaft connects the turbine to the propeller.

ballast tank

High-pressure air is released from these bottles to force water out of the ballast tanks.

The stern (rear) diving planes adjust the depth and angle of diving.

"It navigates the watery deep all by itself: no storms to brave, because just a few meters beneath the waves, it finds absolute tranquillity!"

Jules Verne (1828–1905)
from his novel **Twenty Thousand Leagues under the Sea**

⊜ DIVING AND SURFACING

To dive, water is taken into the submarine's ballast tanks. This makes it heavier so that it sinks. When the crew wants to surface, compressed air forces the water out of the ballast tanks so that the submarine becomes light enough to float on the surface. An Ohio-class submarine is 2,750 tons heavier when submerged than when it is surfaced.

submarine submerging, or diving

submarine emerging, or surfacing

SOLAR FARMING

"The Sun does not shine for a few trees and flowers, but the wide world's joy."

Henry Ward Beecher (1813–1887)
American clergyman

Pure sunlight is the most renewable and unpolluting source of energy, so more and more is being done to try to harness it. One way of generating enormous heat is to magnify, or concentrate, the Sun's rays into one intense beam. Solar farms make good use of this idea. The heat they create and channel is used to generate electricity in a variety of ways. In the future, the world's deserts could become the providers of cheap and environmentally friendly power.

STIRLING ENGINE

A Stirling engine works on the principle that gas expands when it is heated and contracts when it is cooled. The Sun's heat is captured and concentrated by mirrors on the engine's cylinder to heat the gas. Inside the closed system of the engine, the heated gas moves between hot and cold cylinders. This moves a piston to turn a crankshaft, which drives the electrical generator.

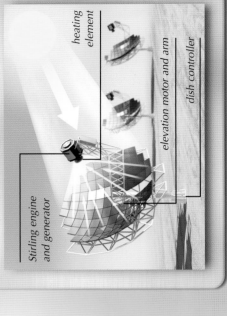

heating element

heliostat array in a desert location

elevation motor and arm

dish controller

Stirling engine and generator

Just 11 sq. ft. (1m²) of reflected sunlight provides enough power to run a small electric fire.

Heliostats

These heliostats are made up of 86 11-sq.-ft. (1m²) mirrors. They are shaped to reflect the sunlight in a concentrated beam onto the heating element of a Stirling engine (see above). One Stirling engine can generate enough electricity to power a family home.

Heliostat mirrors, which can be made of any reflective material, are much cheaper to make and maintain than complicated solar, or photoelectric, panels.

> HELIOSTAT—*a system of mirrors that tracks the position of the Sun, concentrating its rays on a fixed point*

A solar plant

The Solar Two plant (below) was built as an experiment in the Mojave Desert, where sunshine is guaranteed. The amazing array of mirrors concentrates the Sun's rays and beams them to a receiver at the top of a central tower. The generating equipment, housed on the ground, produces enough electricity to power almost 3,000 homes.

1,926 heliostats cover an area of 890,714 sq. ft. (82,750m²), or more than 15 football fields.

A large tank stores hot salt before it flows to the heat exchanger.

turbine and electricity generator

SUPERSALT

The receiver contains hundreds of small tubes filled with molten salt. The concentrated sunshine heats the salt to 1,922°F (1,050°C). It then moves down to a heat exchanger, where it boils water into steam. The steam drives a turbine to generate electricity, and the salt returns to the top of the tower to be reheated.

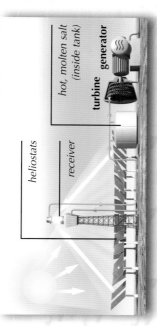

heliostats

receiver

hot, molten salt (inside tank)

turbine generator

> The mirrors of a solar furnace can create a temperature of 5,400°F (3,000°C), half as hot as the Sun.

SOLAR SAILING

Scientists are working on a craft that will be powered by nothing but sunlight. Particles radiating from the Sun put a very tiny amount of pressure on anything they reach—and this is enough, in the vacuum of space, to move an object. A spacecraft with a large-enough solar sail to catch the radiation could voyage to the end of the solar system, and beyond, using no fuel at all.

"We can build sails to catch the radiation blowing from the Sun."

Arthur C. Clarke (1917–2008)
British science-fiction author and inventor

Photons

A beam of sunlight contains uncountable numbers of tiny particles of energy called photons. When sunlight falls on an object, the impact of each photon exerts a minute amount of pressure. Added together, these impulses should push the sail forward.

NanoSail-D

Scientists at NASA have designed an experimental space sail to help them measure the amount of solar pressure required to move things in space. The sail is made of reflective aluminum foil stretched across a frame of strong, lightweight plastic—but it is much too small to power a spacecraft.

NanoSail-D is 100 sq. ft. (9.3m² in area, weighs only 10 lbs. (4.5kg), and can fit inside a small suitcase.

> PHOTON—*a particle of electromagnetic radiation that moves at the speed of light*

Solar spy plane

A solar-powered airplane is perfect for surveying, mapping, or spying on an area. It can fly very high, where there is the most sunlight, and because it flies so slowly—about as fast as you can pedal a bicycle—it can fly over one spot for hours or days at a time. This makes it much cheaper than a space satellite.

solar-powered **Zephyr** aircraft (above)

Two-bladed propellers are designed to work high up, where the air is very thin.

Lightweight materials amount to only 2,050 lbs. (930kg)—about the same weight as a small car.

Solar-powered motors

Fourteen electric motors line the front edge of the giant wing. Each weighs only 11 lbs. (5kg) but has the same power as about five bicycles being pedaled. The electricity is fed to each motor by a cable from either the solar cells or the onboard batteries.

NASA's *Helios* aircraft

Helios is the largest and most powerful solar-powered aircraft yet to fly. The flight was only an experiment and the plane carried no crew, but it reached a record height of 19 mi. (30km). Only rockets and rocket-powered planes have gone higher. The top of the huge, 246-ft. (75-m)-long wing is covered with 62,000 solar cells, which receive light from above and below to maximize their output. Batteries provide backup power in dark or cloudy conditions.

❯ To propel a one-person spacecraft through space, a solar sail would need to be about 2 sq. mi. (5km²) in size.

GPS

Without satellites, modern telecommunication and broadcasting would be impossible. Satellites are also used for spying and to collect data about space and Earth. One of their most useful jobs, though, is to provide the Global Positioning System (GPS). This has revolutionized navigation. Anybody holding a GPS receiver can know, to the nearest yard, exactly where they are on the surface of the planet.

TRILATERATION—the process of fixing a point by knowing the distance from three other points

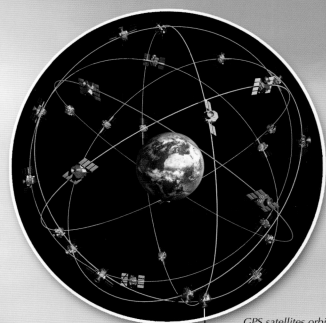

GPS satellites orbit at a height of about 11,000 mi. (18,000km).

a hand-held, portable GPS receiver (below)

GPS satellites

Circling around the world are at least 24 GPS satellites operated by the U.S. Air Force. Each takes 12 hours to orbit (circle) Earth. The first were launched in 1978, and the GPS system was fully operational by 1995.

GPS receivers

As long as it can pick up a signal from three satellites, a GPS receiver can fix a position by trilateration (*see box*). A small computer can then determine the position in latitude and longitude and even convert it to an exact grid reference on a map.

 > The latest cell phones have GPS receivers so that the emergency services know exactly where you are when you call them.

Automatic navigation

Before radio and GPS, ships' navigators and aircraft pilots had to fix their position using the Sun, stars, lights, or landmarks and then figure out a route and make regular checks. A satellite navigation ("sat nav") system continually fixes position and uses a computer to calculate the route and make corrections. The software knows where dangers are and plans a course to avoid them.

www.sciencemuseum.org.uk/onlinestuff/stories/atomic_clocks.aspx

In-car navigators

Drivers use GPS receivers combined with a computer and a digitalized map system. The software stores data of road maps and routes. The GPS location is fed into the computer, which displays the correct part of the map.

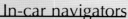

Atomic clock

GPS satellites each contain the most accurate of time-measuring devices—the atomic clock. This ensures that they are all perfectly synchronized (in time with one another) as they emit their signals.

"Knowing exactly where you are now is more than half the secret of getting somewhere else."

**Captain James Weddell
(1787–1834)**
British naval navigator and explorer

The receiver knows the position of the car, and its software can give the driver accurate directions.

TRILATERATION: FIXING POSITION

Each GPS satellite transmits a tracking signal at exactly the same time. A receiver on the ground picks up the signals and determines the distance of each satellite. It plots the closest satellite's position on the surface of an imaginary sphere. The same thing happens with the next two satellites, so three imaginary spheres are created. The spot where all three spheres meet is the true position of the object on the ground that is being tracked.

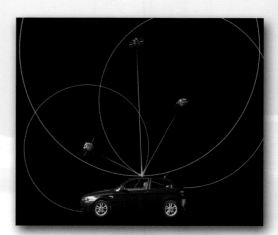

To plot the height of the object above the ground, a fourth satellite signal is needed.

ECOHOME

Houses such as this one are designed to save energy and be kind to the environment. A typical house built in the 1960s had large windows, very little insulation, and central heating that was not carefully controlled. In the 1990s, architects began to plan buildings that used natural energy to the full, created very little waste, and did not harm the atmosphere by giving off greenhouse gases.

Solar power

The Sun's rays provide energy that is clean, nonpolluting, and fairly reliable. They heat and light this house during the day and create extra electricity for it in a row of photoelectric cells, or solar panels.

antireflective glass cover

contact grid

uncharged silicon

positively charged silicon

Photoelectric cells consist of two layers of silicon. When sunlight falls on the top layer, it makes electrons move down to the bottom layer. This creates electricity.

⊖ ENERGY EFFICIENCY

A house in the 1960s needed a lot of energy to keep it warm because almost 50 percent of the heat escaped from its walls, windows, floor, and roof. A passive house loses nine times less heat through the windows, eight times less through the walls, and an amazing 17 times less through the roof. Overall, it is about 11 times more energy efficient.

energy-efficient passive house

typical house from the 1960s

0 1 2 3 4 5 6 7 8 9 10

Heat loss is measured in U-values, with 0 being the most efficient and 10 the least.

The glass has a special coating to reflect heat back into the house.

Two or three layers of glass, with gas in between, protect against heat loss.

> In a well-designed stove, a log can burn for six times as long as it will in an open grate.

A streamlined vane ensures that the turbine always faces the wind.

A turbine with 3-ft. (1-m)-long blades can generate up to 300 kilowatts of power.

Wind turbine

This small turbine, driven by the wind, generates enough electricity to power a kettle and light the whole house. Some of the current is stored in batteries, to be used when there is no wind.

Passive house

A passive house does not actively consume power. This one is built on a site that makes the most use of the Sun for light and warmth. It has superinsulated walls, windows, and roof and is airtight to prevent heat from leaking out and cold air from sneaking in. Most passive houses need only a wood stove or small heat pump to boost the indoor temperature on the coldest days (*see Geothermal heating, below*). The heat pump works in reverse in the summer to cool the house.

www.greeninnovation.co.uk

geothermal heating pipes

Super insulation

Modern insulation materials stop heat from passing from through them. If windows are triple glazed, the walls filled with plastic foam, and the roof space covered with a thick blanket of insulating material, very little heat will be lost.

A 10-in. (25-cm) gap between the outer and inner walls is filled with expanded polystyrene.

Living roof

Instead of using tiles or concrete, a green—or "living"—roof is made of a layer of soil containing growing plants. It keeps the house quiet and helps control its temperature. The plants also absorb carbon dioxide from the air.

underfloor heating system

Geothermal heating

To heat or cool the house, a liquid is pumped through pipes buried in the ground. In the winter, the soil is warmer than the liquid and heats it. In the summer, the soil temperature cools down the warmer liquid.

A pump moves the "refrigerant liquid" around the system.

330 ft. (100m) of plastic pipes, linked to the house, buried 1.5m–2m in the ground.

DIGIWORLD

"Mary had a little lamb."

Thomas Edison (1847–1931)
*American inventor, speaking the
first words ever to be recorded
and played back, in 1877*

In the late 1800s, the inventor Thomas Edison realized
that he could record the shape of sound waves with a
needle by cutting grooves into wax. Recorded sound
completely changed the way people listened to music
in the early 1900s, and there was a second revolution
in the 1980s when recording went digital. These days,
sound can be recorded at much higher quality, in much
greater quantities, and in increasingly small formats.

needle, or stylus,
on a vinyl record

Analogue recording
The wiggly grooves of a record mimic the
form of the original sound wave. The electric
needle in the pickup runs through the grooves
and creates an electrical wave, which is then
converted by the loudspeaker into sounds.

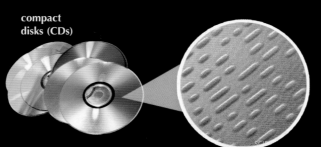

compact
disks (CDs)

Digital recording
In digital recording, the original sound wave
is converted into a numerical code. The high
part of the wave has the highest number and
the low part the lowest. This code is etched
onto a disk as a series of dots and dashes.

> If you listened 24 hours a day for your whole life, you still would not hear all the music that has been recorded.

DIGITAL FILE—a collection of small packages of information stored in a computer's memory

The numbers from sampled sound waves are written in binary code. Binary is a way of writing numbers with just two digits—0 and 1. For example, the number one is written 001, two is 010, and three is 011. This is ideal for digital electronics where switches have only two positions—on and off.

MP3 synchronization

Computer software can convert the tracks on a CD into a file format known as MP3. The MP3 files can then be transferred to an MP3 player or a cell phone so that people can listen to them while on the move.

Storing digital files

Digital music files, such as MP3s or MP4s, can be used to store many hours of music in a tiny space. The music files that contain the information are compressed so that they use up less memory on the music player's digital hard drive.

Apple iPod entertainment system

The player has software that can read the shrunken files and convert them back to audio files.

www.pbs.org/wgbh/amex/edison/sfeature/songs.html

INFORMATION IN A SMALLER SPACE

To get 1,000 hours of recorded sound on the vinyl analogue format, you would need a stack of 1,000 records about 16 ft. (5m) high, weighing about 880 lbs. (400kg). The same amount of information on CD would make a pile of disks 5 ft. (1.5m) high and 44 lbs. (20kg) in weight. A portable MP3 player can hold the same amount of data but is only 0.2 in. (5mm) thick and 0.5 oz. (15g) in weight.

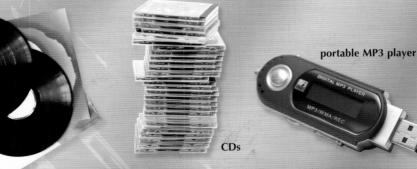

vinyl records

CDs

portable MP3 player

ROBOT RESCUE

Robots are often used to do jobs in situations that are too dangerous for people—such as clearing land mines, studying active volcanoes, and exploring other planets. It is also possible to build computer-controlled battlefield robots to carry out military tasks in locations close to an opposing army, or to rescue wounded soldiers without risking other human lives.

Soldier's friend

Robots such as this one are being developed to rescue wounded soldiers lying where it is too dangerous for medics to go. Remotely controlled, its tracks can cross rough ground. Its "head" contains a camera and sensors for locating casualties. Jointed arms can pull a soldier away from danger along a safe route detected by another set of sensors on its body.

remote-controlled camera

radio antenna

Tiny tank

This small robot can perform jobs such as spying and bomb disposal. Its tracks carry it over rough ground, sand, and snow and through water. It can even climb stairs. An operator controls it by radio from a safe distance.

Tracks are driven by a battery-powered electric motor.

> The word *robota* is Czech for "forced labor." There are about 1.5 million industrial robots working throughout the world.

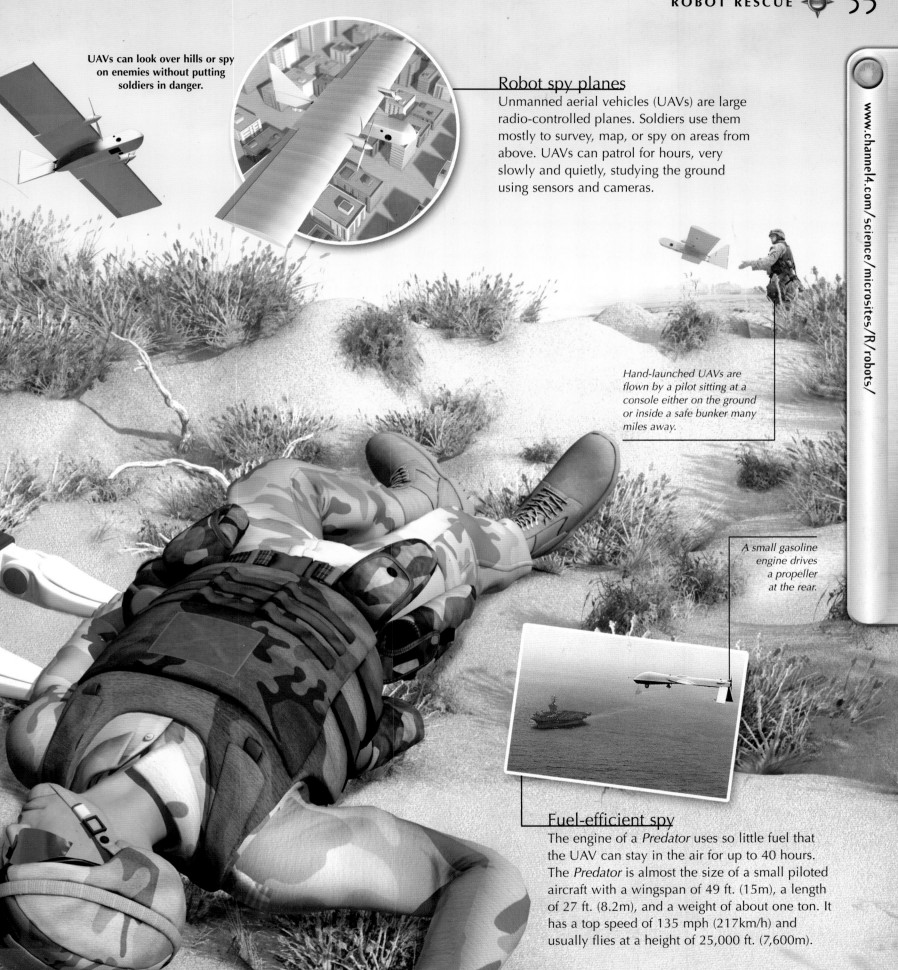

UAVs can look over hills or spy on enemies without putting soldiers in danger.

Robot spy planes

Unmanned aerial vehicles (UAVs) are large radio-controlled planes. Soldiers use them mostly to survey, map, or spy on areas from above. UAVs can patrol for hours, very slowly and quietly, studying the ground using sensors and cameras.

Hand-launched UAVs are flown by a pilot sitting at a console either on the ground or inside a safe bunker many miles away.

A small gasoline engine drives a propeller at the rear.

Fuel-efficient spy

The engine of a *Predator* uses so little fuel that the UAV can stay in the air for up to 40 hours. The *Predator* is almost the size of a small piloted aircraft with a wingspan of 49 ft. (15m), a length of 27 ft. (8.2m), and a weight of about one ton. It has a top speed of 135 mph (217km/h) and usually flies at a height of 25,000 ft. (7,600m).

www.channel4.com/science/microsites/R/robots/

NANOBOTS

As technology progresses, machines become more powerful. Often, they also become much smaller. The first computers were the size of buses, but there is now many, many times more computer power inside a single cell telephone. Nanotechnology is the science of making working machines so small that you can see them only with a microscope. Nanoscience is in its infancy, but when it is perfected, it will change the world as much as did the discovery of electricity or the invention of computers.

MICRON—one-millionth of a meter (this page is approximately 200 microns thick)

Nanorobots may move around by "swimming," using long legs copied from living bacteria.

This nanobot measures only 0.5–3 microns across.

computer model of a part for a nanomachine

Molecular construction

Building nanomachines involves working with tiny pieces of material made up of individual molecules, each consisting of around six atoms. The atoms and molecules can be arranged to form tiny components of amazingly small devices.

Each ball on the model represents a single atom.

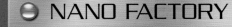

⊖ NANO FACTORY

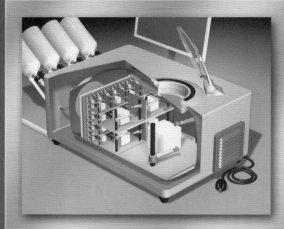

Soon, it might be possible to have a portable "nanofactory," small enough to fit on a desk. Tiny machines inside the device would join together molecules and build them up into larger and larger parts (shown here as white cubes) for use in computers and other electrical equipment.

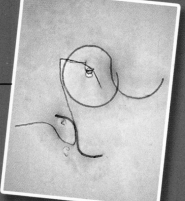

Tiny tubes

Carbon atoms can be formed into tube-shaped molecules, which are fitted together to form nanotubes. These can be used to conduct an electrical current or as tiny mechanical parts in a machine. The largest are only 0.04 in. (1mm) long, but they are ten times stronger than steel.

www.sciencemuseum.org.uk/antenna/nano

"How I long to have the means to explore the teeming worlds I view through my microscope."

Carl Linnaeus (1707–1778)
Swedish scientist

Nanobots in medicine

Someday tiny robots, smaller than grains of salt, could be injected into humans and animals to treat diseases. They would carry drugs directly to the cells that needed them or repair damage deep inside veins, arteries, and organs. In the distant future, people might have medical nanorobots permanently inside them, checking the body for signs of illness and taking action at once.

**mobile cell repairer
nanorobot (below)**

chemical sensors for checking and identifying the target cells

manipulating arm, with gripper for holding on to individual cells

Tiny claws, chisels, and drills would be used to work on diseased tissue.

A tiny computer, inside the nanobot, might be used to navigate around the body.

main probe or manipulator

The machine body is made up of carbon molecules and other diamondlike substances.

Injecting cells

In normal drug treatment, large amounts of chemicals are used to make sure the sick cells are reached. This can damage healthy cells and cause side effects. Using a tiny probe, a nanobot would be able to pierce only the diseased cells, injecting just the right amount of the appropriate drug.

red blood cell inside a human artery

The nanobot might use electrodes, high-frequency microwaves, or ultrasound to kill off dangerous cancer cells.

The power to operate the nanobot might come from a tiny battery or from a motor driven by the natural glucose and oxygen in the body.

∨ RENDERING—in movies and design, this is the process of adding layers and textures to make an object appear realistic

SFX

Film is the only form of art or entertainment that can make the most fantastic and wildest imaginings seem real. Only movies can show battling spaceships, giant waves destroying cities, and hordes of evil monsters on the rampage. Such scenes are created using expensive special effects (SFX) that deceive the eye. Filmmakers used crude special effects 100 years ago, but a truly realistic appearance has been possible only since the invention of computers.

Blue-screen filming

This is a technique that allows the director to make the actors appear in spectacular or impossible situations. First the actors are filmed in front of a blue or bright green screen. Separately, a background scene is filmed, and then, using either computers or special filters, the two pieces of film are joined together so that the actors move realistically in front of the scenery.

The plain green shapes will be rendered by a computer program, which adds skin and hair textures to make them look lifelike.

scene from the movie
***King Kong* (2005)**

⊜ SCALE MODELS

Often it is too expensive and difficult to build a full-size setting for a movie. Carefully made, highly detailed models stand in as scaled-down versions of the real thing. Clever lighting and computer enhancement make it virtually impossible to notice what is a model and what is real.

This model of a capsized U.S. World War II battleship is about one-third of the actual size.

In the studio
The stars of the movie act their part in the studio using props that will be matched and blended into the special effects and live action. This actress (above) is playing her role inside a model that stands in for the giant ape King Kong's thumb and index finger.

 ⟩ To make the 2005 version of *King Kong*, $35 million was spent on special effects alone.

Creature animation

In the past, creature models were animated by filming them frame by frame, re-posing the models slightly in each one. Filmmakers now use computer graphics to create natural-looking creatures, which move and behave as if alive.

Actor sits on a marked area that, on film, will become the polar bear's back.

Virtual lines, joining all the key measuring points on the body, create a 3-D grid, or wire frame, of the bear's body (right).

Wire frame technology

After the designers have sketched the creature, an animator creates a virtual body in the form of a flexible 3-D grid made up of many polygons (shapes). These map out the contours of the body with great accuracy.

First, the actors (below) play the scene in a studio, in front of a blue screen.

When the background is added (above), they appear to be riding in a train through Paris.

Adding backgrounds

As a background, film or computer-generated images can be joined to the blue-screen footage. Then both sequences are transferred, or rendered, to a computer file. The computer software makes sure all the shadows and lighting match and that

"The secret to film is that it's an illusion."

George Lucas (born 1944)
American movie director, producer, and screenwriter, creator of the Star Wars movies

GRAPHIC GAMES

ANIMATION—the illusion of movement created by a rapid sequence of individual frames (pictures), each with slight differences

Making the characters in a computer game takes a lot of imagination, skill, and enormous amounts of sophisticated computer programming. Thinking of the characters and deciding what they look like comes first. Turning the ideas into an onscreen reality, and making them move around, is more about computer science and mathematics.

Creating the exoskeleton

Once a character is finalized on paper, the animator creates a virtual skeleton for it. This is made up of a 3-D grid net that outlines the body. This external covering, or exoskeleton, is basically a digital version of the jointed, posable wooden figures used by traditional artists.

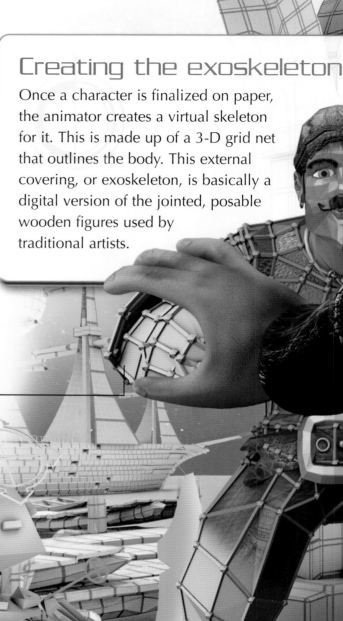

The surface layer of the exoskeleton is built up gradually.

A polygon mesh, made up of shapes, forms the basic exoskeleton.

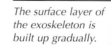

Anchor points on the exoskeleton decide the arrangement of the polygon mesh.

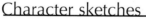

Character sketches

Before any computer programming work is done, the characters are developed the old-fashioned way—by drawing. This is the stage for experimenting with all the details and colors of faces, hairstyles, and clothing.

Anchor points

These are the points where parts of the body will revolve, turn, or balance to form its key movements. The computer is programmed to know how the joints work, and how heavy the limbs are, so that it can create realistic movements.

Hinges, or avars, are added to the exoskeleton—usually where the body's natural joints would be.

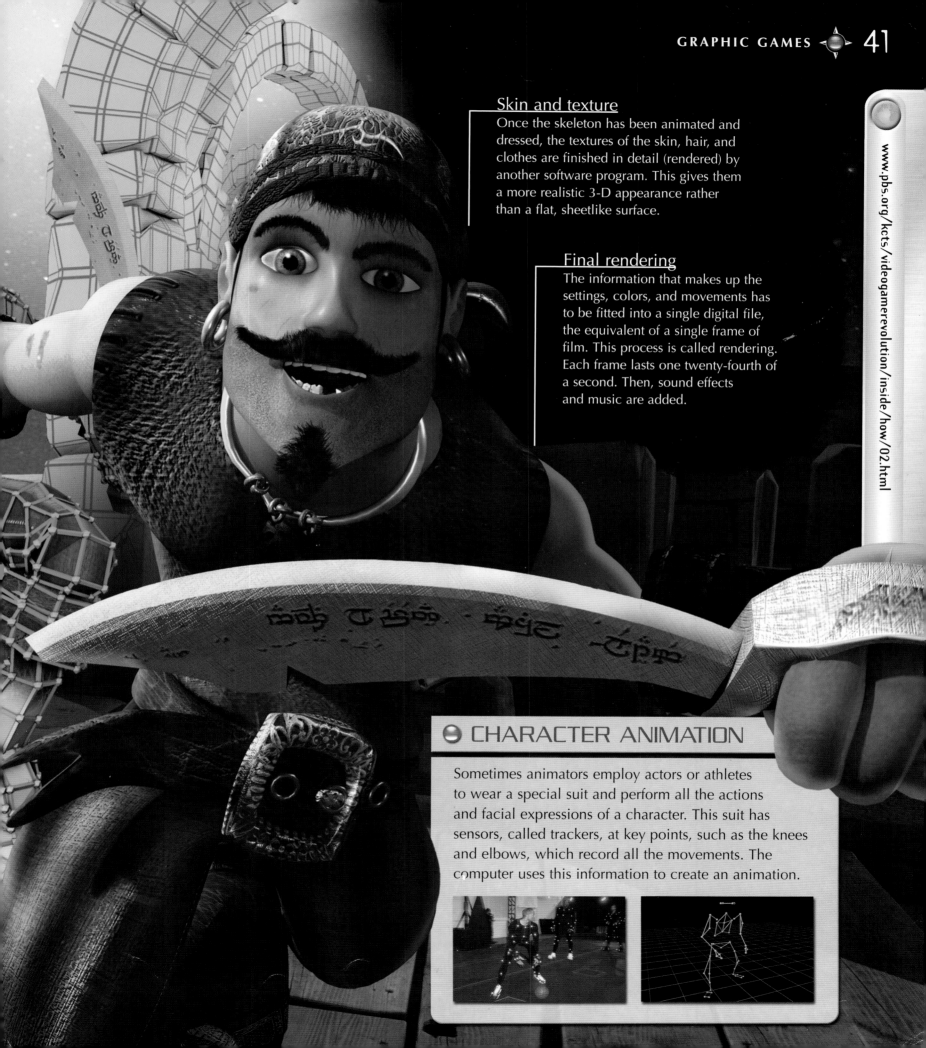

www.pbs.org/kcts/videogamerevolution/inside/how/02.html

Skin and texture

Once the skeleton has been animated and dressed, the textures of the skin, hair, and clothes are finished in detail (rendered) by another software program. This gives them a more realistic 3-D appearance rather than a flat, sheetlike surface.

Final rendering

The information that makes up the settings, colors, and movements has to be fitted into a single digital file, the equivalent of a single frame of film. This process is called rendering. Each frame lasts one twenty-fourth of a second. Then, sound effects and music are added.

⊜ CHARACTER ANIMATION

Sometimes animators employ actors or athletes to wear a special suit and perform all the actions and facial expressions of a character. This suit has sensors, called trackers, at key points, such as the knees and elbows, which record all the movements. The computer uses this information to create an animation.

POLYURETHANE—a hard, dense plastic material invented in 1937

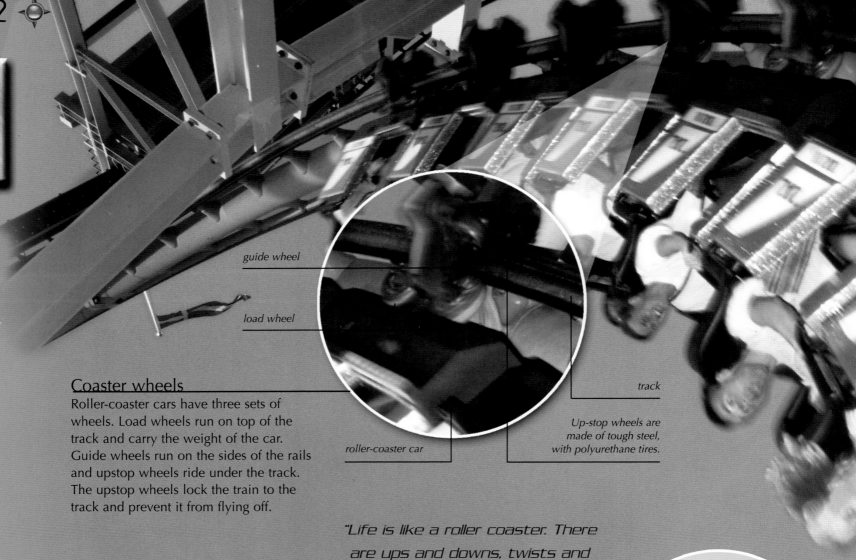

guide wheel

load wheel

track

Coaster wheels

Roller-coaster cars have three sets of wheels. Load wheels run on top of the track and carry the weight of the car. Guide wheels run on the sides of the rails and upstop wheels ride under the track. The upstop wheels lock the train to the track and prevent it from flying off.

roller-coaster car

Up-stop wheels are made of tough steel, with polyurethane tires.

"Life is like a roller coaster. There are ups and downs, twists and turns . . . unless you fall off."

Traditional saying

FUN MACHINE

Technology is not just for the serious side of life. It also gives us the roller coaster—a machine good for nothing but thrills, hurling us on a spectacular, stomach-churning ride to nowhere. Pure fun! Roller coasters first appeared in Russia as sleds on icy slides. These became popular in France—but because France is warmer than Russia, the ice melted. Someone had the idea of attaching wheels to the sleds and then fitting those wheels onto a track—and so the roller coaster was born.

Centrifugal force

This force overcomes gravity and holds the cars and their passengers on the track as they loop the loop. As the cars accelerate, they want to fly off in a straight line but are forced into a curve by the track. This creates the centrifugal force, which presses and holds the cars against the track.

> There are almost 2,100 roller coasters operating worldwide.

www.funderstanding.com/coaster

⊖ FAIRGROUND FORCES

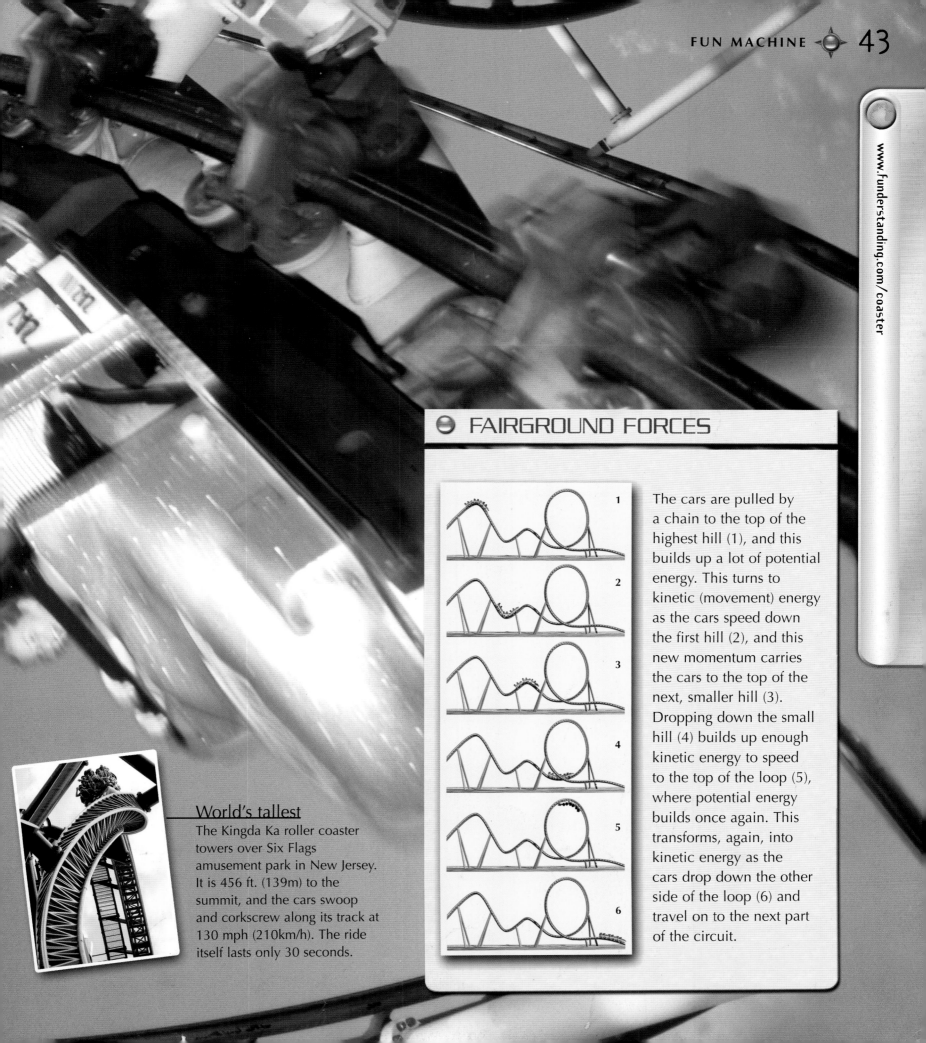

The cars are pulled by a chain to the top of the highest hill (1), and this builds up a lot of potential energy. This turns to kinetic (movement) energy as the cars speed down the first hill (2), and this new momentum carries the cars to the top of the next, smaller hill (3). Dropping down the small hill (4) builds up enough kinetic energy to speed to the top of the loop (5), where potential energy builds once again. This transforms, again, into kinetic energy as the cars drop down the other side of the loop (6) and travel on to the next part of the circuit.

World's tallest

The Kingda Ka roller coaster towers over Six Flags amusement park in New Jersey. It is 456 ft. (139m) to the summit, and the cars swoop and corkscrew along its track at 130 mph (210km/h). The ride itself lasts only 30 seconds.

GLOSSARY

3-D
Three dimensional—describes an object that has height, width, and depth.

acceleration
The act of speeding up or also, in machines, the ability to speed up.

analogue
Describes a device that reproduces data as a continuously changing stream of information rather than digitally.

atmosphere
The layer of gases that surrounds a planet such as Earth.

atom
The smallest particle of a chemical element. An element is a pure substance that is made of only one type of atom.

axle
A rod or spindle that passes through the center of a wheel, around which the wheel turns.

centrifugal force
A force that acts on something traveling on a circular path, pushing it away from the center of that circle.

climate
The average weather of a location over a period of time.

crankshaft
An axle (or shaft) that is driven by turning a handle (or crank).

elevon
On the wings of an aircraft, a surface that the pilot can move up or down to adjust the craft's pitch (nose up or nose down) and to stop it from rolling.

fission
The splitting of an atom to release nuclear energy.

gear
A toothed wheel that meshes with other toothed wheels to create a driving force.

generator
A machine that transforms movement energy into electricity.

gravity
The force of attraction between two objects. On Earth, gravity pulls objects toward the center of the planet and stops them from floating off into space.

hard drive
The part of a computer used for storing digital data.

horsepower
A unit for measuring engine power, based on how much of the same work a horse could do. One unit of horsepower is equal to 750 watts of power.

jack
A device for lifting heavy equipment. Pneumatic jacks are powered by compressed air.

kinetic energy
The extra energy an object has when it is moving.

laser
A device that produces a very thin and powerful beam of light.

microwave
An invisible form of energy, similar to light, used for cooking and communication.

molecule
A group of two or more atoms bonded together.

momentum

The force that an object gathers as it moves and which keeps it moving.

navigation

Finding the way or charting a course.

orbit

The path of one object around another object in space.

payload

The cargo carried inside a vehicle.

photoelectric cell

Also called a solar cell. A type of tile, usually made of specially-treated silicon, that collects sunlight and transforms it into electrical energy.

potential energy

The possible energy stored inside an object owing to its position (for example, a raised pendulum) or its condition (for example, a charged battery).

ram

A device that puts pressure on something in order to drive it into a particular place.

renewable

Describes a resource or fuel that can be used without it running out for future generations, because it can be replaced naturally or with careful management.

satellite

Anything that goes around, or orbits, something else. Artificial (human-made) satellites traveling around Earth are used in communications.

sensor

A device that can detect a particular kind of stimulus such as heat, light, sound, or movement.

software

Also known as programs—the complex instructions used in computer systems, enabling a computer to perform specific functions.

sound wave

The means by which noise travels through air, water, or the ground as a series of vibrations (shaking movements).

stage (of a rocket)

One of the two or more separate sections of a rocket, each of which has its own fuel and engine.

synchronization

Putting things in time with one another.

thrust

The force that pushes something onward.

turbine

A machine that is used to change movement energy—from flowing water or steam—into a turning motion that powers machinery (such as a generator).

ultrasound

A type of sound wave, outside the range of human hearing, that can be bounced off an unseen object in order to form an image of it.

virtual

Artificially created by a computer.

weightlessness

The experience of being beyond the pull of gravity, such as in space. (Weight is the measurement of how much the force of gravity acts on an object.)

INDEX

A

acceleration 10, 42, 44
airplanes 5, 9, 10, 27, 29,
    35
AGV trains 11
analogue recordings 32,
    33, 44
anchor points 40
animation 39, 40, 41
aquabuoys 19
atmosphere 12, 15, 17,
    30, 44
atomic clocks 29
atoms 12, 20, 36, 44
axles 10, 44

B

ballast tanks 22, 23
batteries 27, 31, 34, 37
BepiColombo 13
binary code 32
blue-screen filming 38, 39
boron 21
bridges 5, 8–9

C

cars 5, 29
cell phones 28, 33, 36
centrifugal force 42, 44

chain reactions 20, 21
climate 4, 44
coal 4
communication 5, 13, 28,
    44, 45
compact disks (CDs) 32,
    33
composites 5
computer games 5, 40–41
computers 22, 28, 29, 32,
    33, 34, 35, 36, 37,
    38–39, 44, 45
concrete 6, 8, 9
cooling towers 21
crankshafts 24, 44
cutter heads 7

DE

digital technology 5,
    32–33, 38–39, 40–41
electricity 4, 5, 11, 13, 16,
    18, 19, 20, 21, 23, 24,
    30, 31, 36, 44, 45
elevons 15, 44
engines 10, 12, 13, 14,
    44, 45

F

fission 20, 21, 44
fossil fuels 4, 5

G

gas, natural 4
gears 10, 44
generators 4, 18, 19, 20,
    21, 24, 25, 44
geothermal power 4, 31
gliding 14, 15
Global Positioning System
    (GPS) 28, 29
Gotthard Base Tunnel 7
gravity 12, 14, 42, 44, 45
greenhouse gases 10, 18,
    20, 30

H

hard drives 33, 44
heating 5, 30, 31
Helios 27
heliostats 24
homes 5, 18, 24, 25,
    30–31, 45
horsepower 10, 44
hydraulic power 8, 9,
    18, 19

IJ

in-car navigators 29
insulation 31
Internet 5, 33

ion engines 13
ions 12
jacks 6, 7, 8, 9, 44
jet engines 14

KL

kinetic energy 43, 44
laser beams 7, 16, 17,
    44

M

medical technology 34,
    37
microns 36
microwaves 37, 44
military technology
    22–23, 27, 28,
    34–35
Millau Viaduct 8–9, 15
molecules 36, 44
momentum 43, 45
movies 38, 39, 48
MP3s 33

NO

nanometers 16
NanoSail-D 26
nanotechnology 36–37
nanotubes 5, 16, 36

natural resources 4
navigation 22, 28–29, 37, 45
neutrons 20, 21
nuclear power
 see particle power
orbits 12, 13, 14, 16, 17, 45

PQ

pantographs 11
particle power 5, 20–21, 22–23, 44, 48
passive houses 30–31
payloads 12, 13, 45
periscopes 22
photoelectric cells 16, 30, 45
photons 26
piers 8, 9
pistons 18, 19, 24
pneumatic power 6, 44
pollution 4
polyurethane 42
potential energy 18, 43, 45
power plants 4, 17, 20–21, 45
propellers (in vehicles) 23, 27

R

radar 22
radio communications 22, 29, 34
radioactivity 20, 26
rail transportation 6, 10–11
rams 6, 19, 45
reactors 20, 21, 22, 23
rendering 38, 40, 41
renewable energy 18, 24, 45
rigs 4
roads 8, 9, 29
robots 34–35, 36–37, 48
rockets 12–13, 14, 15, 17, 45
roller coasters 42–43
rudders 15, 23

S

satellites 5, 12, 14, 17, 27, 28–29, 45
sensors 34, 35, 37, 41, 45
software 29, 33, 39, 41, 45
solar cells 27
 see also photoelectric cells
solar farms 24–25
solar panels 13, 24

solar power 5, 24–25, 26–27, 30
solar sails 26–27
Solar Two plant 24
sonar 22
sound recording 32–33
sound waves 32, 45
Soyuz-Fregat rockets 12
space elevators 16–17
space stations 14, 16, 17
space transportation 12–17, 26–27
spacecraft 5, 12–13, 14–15, 16, 26–27
spaceports 15
SpaceShipTwo 14, 15
special effects (SFX) 38–39
spying 27, 28, 34, 35
stages, rocket 12, 45
steel 7, 8, 9, 21
Stirling engines 24
submarines 20, 22–23
synchronization 29, 33, 45

T

TGV trains 10–11
three-dimensionality (3D) 39, 40, 41, 44
thrust 13, 45
trains, high-speed 10–11
transformers 11

trilateration 28, 29
tunnel-boring machines (TBMs) 6, 7
tunnels 5, 6–7
turbines 4, 19, 20, 21, 23, 25, 31, 45

UV

ultrasound 37, 45
unmanned aerial vehicles (UAVs) 35
uranium 20, 21
U-values 30
vehicles 5, 10–11, 12–13, 14–15, 22–23, 26–27, 29, 34, 35, 44, 45

W

water power 4, 18–19
wave farms 4, 18–19
wedges 9
weightlessness 14, 15, 45
wheels 10, 11, 42, 44
wheel trucks 10, 11
wind power 5, 18, 31

XYZ

X Prize 14
xenon 13

INVESTIGATE

Get in touch with technology by visiting museums and other places of interest—and don't forget to keep up with the news!

Museums and exhibitions

One of the best ways to learn about new technology, and play around with it, is to visit museums and exhibitions close to where you live.

WALL-E (2008) is an animated movie set in the future, featuring a lovable waste-collecting robot.

 Wow! Inventions That Changed the World by Philip Ardagh (Macmillan Children's Books)

 Technology Gallery, The New York Hall of Science, 47-01 111th Street, Queens, NY 11368

www.tryscience.org

A child plays with a robot during the Robot World exhibition in Taiwan.

Film and fiction

Sometimes science-fiction writers and artists come up with ideas and inventions in books and movies which are later developed and used in real life.

 Out of This World: Science-Fiction Stories chosen by Edward Blishen (Kingfisher)

 Forbidden Planet (a chain of science-fiction stores) 179 Shaftesbury Avenue, London WC2H 8JR, U.K.

www.wall-e.com

The president of Panasonic answers questions about his company's state-of-the-art products.

TV and the news

New technology is talked about on TV news bulletins or in magazine, newspaper, and Internet articles. So keep your eyes open, or get an adult to save the articles for you!

 Yes Mag (Canadian science magazine for kids)

 Nick News (news program for children)

www.nick.com/nicknews

A visitor takes pictures during an open day at the European Laboratory for Particle Physics in Geneva, Switzerland.

Tours and visits

Some industrial plants, power plants, and factories—normally closed to the public—offer special tours for schools or have visitor centers that show you what goes on inside.

  Physics: Why Matter Matters! by Dan Green and Simon Basher (Kingfisher)

  American Whistle Corporation, 6540 Huntley Road, Columbus, OH 43229

 www.benjerry.com/scoop-shops/factory-tours/

FEB   2010